Tom Mathews was born in Dublin in 1952. After working in advertising he studied Fine Art at NCAD, since leaving which in 1975 he has worked as a freelance cartoonist, writer and critic. His work appears regularly in *The Irish Times* and *Sunday Independent,* as well as in *Hotpress* and other magazines. He has had twenty one-man shows and his paintings have been exhibited in The Living Art, National Portrait Show and the R.H.A. He has illustrated a dozen books, written a novel and published two collections of cartoons. His work is in many national and international collections. His hobbies are drinking stout, writing verse and talking too much about Groucho Marx and James Joyce.

Tom Mathews

the best of

NEW
ISLAND

Copyright © 2005 Tom Mathews

THE BEST OF TOM MATHEWS
First published 2005
by New Island
2 Brookside
Dundrum Road
Dublin 14

www.newisland.ie

ISBN 1 904301 79 7

British Library Cataloguing in Publication Data.
A CIP catalogue record for this book is available
from the British Library.

Typeset by New Island
Cover design by New Island
Printed in Spain by Edelvives

To ten good friends and true whose company has generated so much laughter over the years: Willie Brennan, Jim Cogan, Barry Doyle, Kevin Byrne, Philip Bellew, James C. Harrold, Naoise Nunn, Eamonn O'Doherty, Gerry Stevenson and Killian O'Donnell; and to nine Muses: Margaret Deignan, Trudy Hayes, Maggie Ryan, Aoibheann Lambe, Francesca Lalor, Liz Ryan, Evanna O'Boyle, Edel Gallagher and Paula Nolan, this book is affectionately dedicated.

My thanks are due to the editors of *The Irish Times*, *Sunday Independent*, *In Dublin Magazine*, *Hotpress*, *Hibernia*, and *The Dubliner*, in whose pages these drawings first appeared.

Foreword

I have been in love with Tom Mathews's work for many years. The simplest reason is that I enjoy a laugh but, as with all good laughs, it is so much more. He moves effortlessly from the straightforward depiction of a ridiculous situation, jibing gently as he goes, to complex matters of the very nature of Art. All the while he remains accessible on whatever level you wish to choose to view his work on any given day. Not only can he cater to the base and the cerebral, his actual execution is so beautiful of itself that I sometimes gasp at his prodigious ability. And his style is instantly recognisable. The dogs on the street would know a Tom Mathews.

As it happens he is also one of the nicest and dearest people you could encounter on a day's walk and one of the last of the true eccentrics we have in the country (but one that you could introduce to someone without offence). Frankly, he is a National Treasure.

I have one of his framed works in my bathroom and therefore think of him every day, and even on the baddest day that cartoon raises a grin. What can I tell you? He makes me laugh and he keeps me regular. Who could ask for anything more?

Pauline McLynn

"STOP MAKING SENSE."

"THAT DIFFICULT SECOND ALBUM"

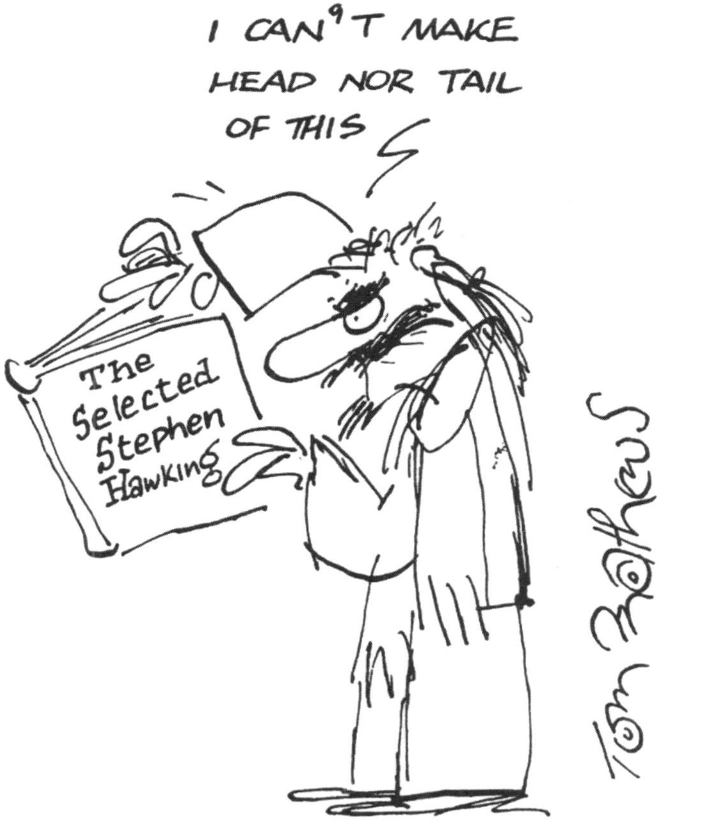

"A brief waste of time."

"THE LONE ARRANGER".

AL SOON WORKED UP A GOOD HEAD OF STEAM

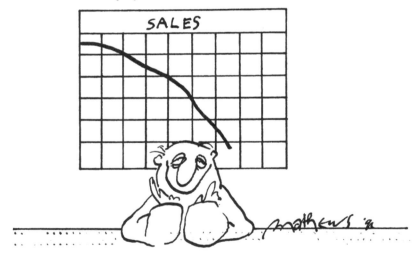

I CAN SEE MYSELF GROWING OLD WITH YOU.

MADAME ASTRA CRYSTAL GAZER

I CAN'T TONIGHT I'M GOING TO HAVE A HEADACHE

SURREALIST CHANGING
A LIGHTBULB.

THE ANCIENT ART OF SELF OFFENCE.

NO WEIGH, JOSÉ.

IRON.

MEN WORKING

MAN WATCHING

Tom Mathews.

MARVO THE MENTALIST

PLEASE TAKE A NUMBER FROM ONE TO TEN

HUP 234

POST

JUNK MAIL

A SOPHISTICATED COUPLE PUTS DOWN ROOTS.

MONOTONY

VOTE LABOUR

"JUST UP AND LEFT"

EMERGENCY PROCEDURES FOR THE INSANE

IN CASE
OF FIRE
BREAK
WIND.

Tom Mathews.

THE SUDDEN BLINDING
REALISATION SWEETSHOP

PENNY
DROPS

Tom Mathews '86.

FISH
SHOP

BRILL!

TIME TRAVEL
EXPERIMENTS
LTD.

I WANT
IT YESTERDAY.

THEATRE OF
CRUELTY.

"GRAND LARSONY"

Tom Mathews

GET THOSE ARMS OFF THE TABLE.

GERRY ADAMS — THE EARLY YEARS.

SHUDDENLY IT ALL MAKESH COMPLETE SHENSE

JOHNATHAN LIVINGSTONE SEAGRAM.

"THE ARTIST FORMERLY KNOWN AS PRINCE."

A RENOWNED SOCIALITE,
GEORGE HAD MANY HANGERS ON.

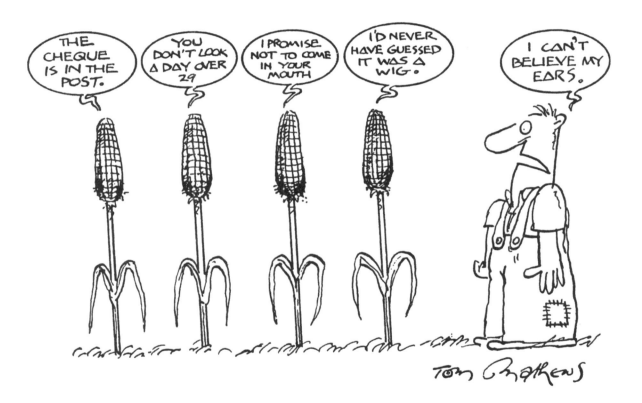

CURSE OF THE TEENAGE WEREWOLF.

"THOSE IRREPRESSIBLE CAVEMEN"

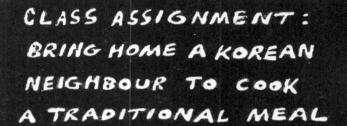

CLASS ASSIGNMENT:
BRING HOME A KOREAN
NEIGHBOUR TO COOK
A TRADITIONAL MEAL

PLEASE MISS,
MY HOMEWORK
ATE THE DOG.

YOURS IS A MYSTERIOUS
ENIGMATIC CHARM
MISS JOHNSON.

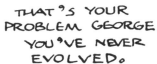

"BIOLOGICAL ALARM CLOCK."

SPEED DATING

DON'T MENTION THE WAR.

"THE SECRET LIFE OF SKIPPY."

I'M TERRIBLY SORRY BUT MY AD SAID I'D LIKE TO MEET AN OLD HIPPY.

"THE SWAN OF AVON"

THAT'S RIGHT — JUST RUN AWAY FROM EVERYTHING.

le Hockney de nos jours.

FOR THIS WE GOT UP EARLY?

Tom Brothers.

"THE NAME'S
ACER PSEUDOPLATANUS
BRILLIANTISSIMUM"
BUT YOU CAN CALL ME "ACE".

Tom Brothers

HAVE AN ICE DAY.

NO MORE WARFARIN

SCREEN II SIDEWAYS

TICKETS

ONE PLEASE.

THERE'S OBVIOUSLY BEEN SOME SORT OF MIX UP AT THE DATING AGENCY

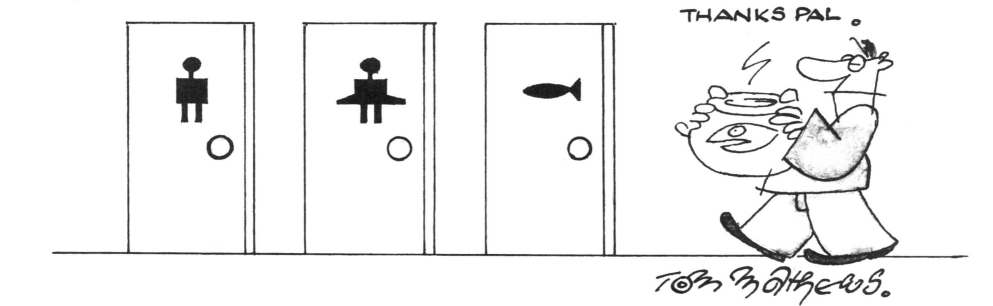

DON'T HAVE
A SIMPSON
MAN.

Tom Mathews '96.

Salad BAR

I'M SORRY SIR YOU'VE HAD ENOUGH

Tom Mathews

'He treats that dog exactly like one of his own family'

GUIDE DOGS FOR THE DEAF

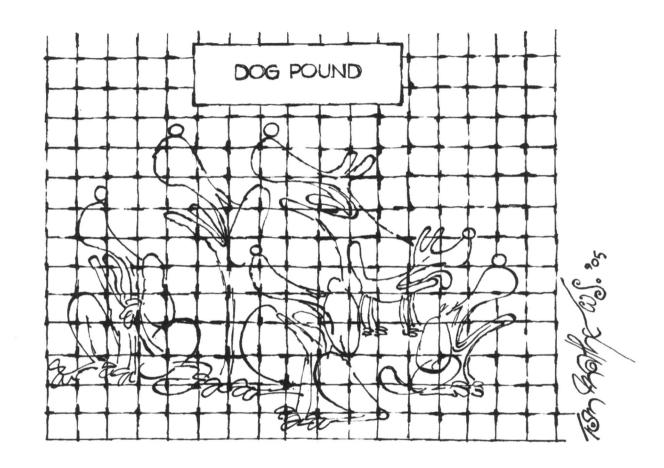

♫ PEOPLE TRY TO PUT US DOWN – JUST BECAUSE WE GET AROUND ♪

"DISGUSTING."

Tom Mathews.

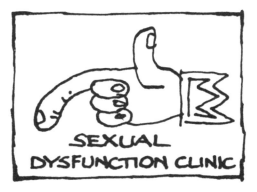

Tom Matthews

THERE'S NOTHING I CAN DO — YOU'RE KRAZY.